MOUTHS
OPEN
TO NAME
HER

Barataria Poetry
AVA LEAVELL HAYMON, *Series Editor*

MOUTHS OPEN TO NAME HER

POEMS

KATIE BICKHAM

LOUISIANA STATE UNIVERSITY PRESS
BATON ROUGE

Published by Louisiana State University Press
Copyright © 2019 by Katie Bickham

All rights reserved
Manufactured in the United States of America
LSU Press Paperback Original

DESIGNER: Mandy McDonald Scallan
TYPEFACE: Sina Nova
PRINTER AND BINDER: LSI

Library of Congress Cataloging-in-Publication Data

Names: Bickham, Katie, author.
Title: Mouths open to name her : poems / Katie Bickham.
Description: Baton Rouge : Louisiana State University Press, [2019]
Identifiers: LCCN 2018035316| ISBN 978-0-8071-6987-2 (pbk. : alk. paper) | ISBN
   978-0-8071-7094-6 (pdf) 978-0-8071-7095-3 (epub)
Classification: LCC PS3602.I283 A6 2019 | DDC 811/.6—dc23
LC record available at https://lccn.loc.gov/2018035316

The paper in this book meets the guidelines for permanence and durability of the Committee on Production Guidelines for Book Longevity of the Council on Library Resources. ∞

for Helen, who has never stopped teaching me
and for Keith, who has waited a long time for a love poem

BABA YAGA:

You have made a creature.
You have made a creature.
You have made a creature.
I know of no happening more strange, mysterious, witchly, frightful, powerful, magical. You are one to fear and admire.

—TAISIA KITAISKAIA

CONTENTS

Doorway

    The Good News 3

Candle

    Berry Picking 7

    Charleston, South Carolina, 1864 8

    Naming 9

    Manhattan, New York, 1970 11

    The Emptiness, Alone 13

    Magdeburg, Germany, 1912 15

    Houma, Louisiana, 1862 16

    Mother and Son in Ash 18

    Nice, France, 1886 19

Weapon

    Shorn 23

    Dublin, Ireland, 1893, 1993 26

    Supply 29

    Los Alamos, New Mexico, 1945 31

    Hiroshima, Japan, 1945 33

    I Know God 35

    Pearl River, Louisiana, 1859 36

    Morning 38

    Tehran, Iran, 1941 39

Edenton, North Carolina, 1968.... 40
Nunavik Region, Quebec, Canada, 1965.... 43
Montgomery, Alabama, 1847.... 45
Buenos Aires, Argentina, 1978.... 47

Ship

Missoula, Montana, 1950.... 51
The Thing They Say Makes Us Love Each Other.... 53
Shreveport, Louisiana, 1986.... 56
Plea.... 57
Serengeti District, Tanzania, 2017.... 58
Unnamed Hamlet, Oaxaca, Mexico, 2004.... 60
At Last, She Is Finished with Emptiness.... 62

Acknowledgments.... 63
Source Materials.... 65

MOUTHS
OPEN
TO NAME
HER

DOORWAY

The Good News

Today, 350,000 babies will be born.
Yesterday, they were all on their way,
almost with us, not here yet,
but today, they will arrive. All of them,
three hundred and fifty thousand of them
in a single sleek rotation of the earth.

Alone and in pairs, screaming and silent,
headfirst and feetfirst, they are coming,
another dozen every second, no matter how
many forests we bulldoze or bullets we fire.
They arrive and arrive like a laugh
we can't stifle even at funerals or faculty meetings,
a cup fuller each time we come for a drink.
No matter how many barrels of oil
we pump from the desert or dump in the ocean,
how many units of blood we transfuse into soldiers,
they arrive and arrive, the good news
we can't wait to tell our buddies, the dog's tail
thumping the carpet at five o'clock, fish and loaves
multiplying in the hands of Christ, unstoppable
even after we push back from the table, full

to bursting. And these are just humans.
What glut of joy to count, as well,
the millions of featherless birds bucking
shells, minnows clumsy in cold currents,
downy puppies with flat noses, or the lowly billion
tomatoes taking root, acorns gaining purchase,
moss doubling on hundred-year-old trees
and the just-as-likely infants on triple-distant moons
orbiting planets we haven't named.

But our home, today, before you fall asleep,
will be 350,000 babies richer, 700,000 lungs louder,
fanned by billions of brand new eyelashes. And if you're low,
if you've watched too much news or fallen
out of love or lost your keys or your faith,
or if all of the sunsets begin to look alike,

just picture them all, 350,000 babies, together at once,
a city's worth of them in a row or a circle or wrapped
in an acres-wide blanket, an army of innocence yawning
their first breaths over the globe, and the promise
that it will all happen again, just like this, just as imperfectly,
no matter what,
tomorrow.

CANDLE

Berry Picking

That summer in liquid heat,
my mother took me berry picking.
We heaped them in tin buckets
to the brim. She was rattling
off her mother's recipe for compote
when it happened.
She noticed first.

What I thought was sweat
dripped down, staining the tiny corn-silk hairs
on my freckled thigh.

I jumped at the sight, fingers desperate
to find the source. My mother
walked away from me, let me understand.
I cupped my hands against myself,
pitiful and sweating. *Momma?*
What's wrong? But she was a stone
in the orchard, face fixed in still
resignation, and nothing else.

My clothes clung to me. I curled—
weeping in the dappled shade,
berries glinting dumbly in the sun.
Why wouldn't she hold me?

this woman who sat vigil for each fever,
who said once that she'd stayed up late
counting the hairs on my head.
Her eyes rooted to my sullied leg,
she knew what I did not:
from that moment on, all the words we said
would loosely translate to goodbye.

Charleston, South Carolina, 1864

Lenore had learned to sew skin before dresses,
dressed combat wounds in scanty light, lit fires with bark
and sheet music. Her first blood soaked

through her homespun dress, camouflaged
by the blood of others. After disease or grief
or their gentle natures did the other women in,

Lenore and another girl, Adelaide, begged
and learned by heart the body's fields and rows,
its floodplains, forests, streams, and even

how to set a bone, pull a tooth. They gave the men—
too tired to note their youth—homemade whiskey
before they cut away ruined skin.

They held their dinner down, breathed through
their mouths, sat vigil and sang Adelaide's work songs.
Girls are good for work like this,

she thought, as Adelaide slept briefly in her arms.
The sun rose on some thousandth day of war,
and she, who'd never seen a baby born, had seen

the other way life goes, the slow or sudden flicker
of the end. The girls would wash each other's faces
in the night, sleep together, quietly agreed

that any good soft secret left unbloodied
ought to be consumed. Girls were good for love
like this, sequestered from the bullet wounds

of war. They smoked tobacco with the soldiers
who could breathe, shared their food, held hands
over the dying and heard their prayers, a woman's work.

Naming

My mother named me when I was the sound
wind made in her youth, the flicker of love
before she fell into it.

My mother named me
before she saw me, before my father came
to make me. Even Adam,
the great namer,
saw the beasts before he burdened them
with names.

When I was a still-growing girl, the name
she chose closed in, ill fitting like clothes
I'd outgrown. I told new manicurists,
tire technicians, barkeeps in other countries
I was Sophia or Helen or Rose,
that my mother named me Genevieve or Julia.
My own name was still a lie
I told, the same as those.

As I grew older, I kept it pared down
like a fingernail—
the single crescent syllable—
the indivisible atom—
the unshakeable Kate.
Sometimes like a child to my mother's
skirts, I dashed back to the given,
Katherine,
to sign a document, to feel full grown.

If I could slip into the menagerie
between tiger and nightingale,
straight and tall and certain of my skin,
what name would Adam call me?

Perhaps names are a house we learn to live in
and then, when traveling,
find ourselves referring to as home.
My mother named me when I was the sound
wind made in her youth.
Some day, when I am old,
I will hear her calling my name in the wind
and I will finally say yes,
that is me,
I am coming.

Manhattan, New York, 1970

The woman's husband had been gone for hours
when she broke. She left the bleating infant
on the Persian rug, backed away from it into the next room,
and slid down the bedroom wall in her silk robe.
Through the closet door, she saw her fine suits hanging

pressed and long unworn. Her breasts were burning, useless.
For three days she had cradled the soft mewling thing
against her, stroked its invisible brows and braced,
prayed as it suckled. God, if he was there, said nothing.
No one did. She was alone with it. The phone was mute.

She howled, too, like an animal, in a contest
with the child, howled at every woman who'd ever
gently nursed her infant in the peaceful early dark,
and only when the knock, the "Señora?"
came from the front room, did she remember

it was Wednesday. There was no time, no time
to run back to pick up the child from the floor, to mop
her eyes before Luisa bustled through the rooms.
Baby cradled in her certain arms, Louisa came into
the bedroom, mouth agape. "Señora, the baby hungers,"

she said. The woman choked her weeping,
shook her head, held herself. "I can't. I can't.
There's something wrong with me," she whispered to the floor.
Luisa came, hitched up her starched gray work dress,
and sat across from the woman, baby screaming

all the time. "Nothing wrong," she said, touching
the woman for the first time—dry hand
on the woman's knee. "I'll help you." Sleep-starved
and half-hating the child she so desperately wanted
to feed, she didn't flinch when Luisa undid buttons,

eased a light-brown breast striped with silvery stretch marks
out of a cotton brassiere, and lifted the baby. The woman,
who had never even asked to see a photo
of Luisa's children, felt the shame of one whose wrongs,
suddenly compiled, are unforgivable. But then her fingers,

on their own, stroked her child at another woman's breast,
and her eyes, now tearless, met Luisa's. She felt
release and the comfort of a wordlessly forgiven sin.
A sound like slurping coffee filled the room.
"Worry stops the milk," Luisa said.

"Picture the hydrant where the childrens play. Imagine
waterfalls. Have you seen waterfalls? Warm rags will help the—Look!"
she said, nodding at the woman's chest. The woman
looked down. Her fine white robe had gone translucent,
warm streams pooling in her lap.

The Emptiness, Alone

In Louisiana, after six years
of marriage, I've heard people whisper
about my childlessness.

People, and my brothers
in their white houses, yards
sprayed with toys. My mother,
who is beginning to look old.

I've never told them, but the lowest
I felt was the two weeks
my husband and I owned
our first house, but
hadn't yet moved in.

I'd visit in the mornings,
the echo of my single key knocking
through the empty rooms.
The first day I took a box
of books, arranged them
on the bare shelves,

climbed and descended the hundred-
year-old stairs to the third-floor bedroom
where we would not
make children.

Each day, I'd take some trinket,
rags to treat the wood, dry goods
to fill the dusty pantry, like a lonesome
castaway trying to civilize
her island.

I don't know what drove me
each afternoon to face the emptiness
alone, but once inside—
sitting in the cold tub with
no water and no curtain

or lying on the creaking floor
in our dining room—
I was sad for the century
the house had stood, the weight
of the yet-uninhabited decades
we might shuffle through those halls.
I felt the great enclosure of my skin,
the cold cavern of my own heart,
and could hardly get a breath.

I've never been nearer my own ending,
but I imagine the uplifted eyes
of our child, its unfurnished soul,
empty as the void,

waiting for me to fill it up, waiting
for me to give it a name, waiting
for me each afternoon to make it
mine.

That would be the end
of any lightness
I have left.

Magdeburg, Germany, 1912

> The night of my confinement will always be a
> night dropped out of my life."
> —MRS. MARK BOYD, *The Ladies World,* 1913

The Americawn woman knew women had withstood
the agony for millennia, but Herr Doktor stood
firm. This was a new world: a blessing, too,

she told herself, not to be home howling by the hearth.
Worth her memories, worth sailing halfway round the earth
was the Dämmerschlaf, the twilight sleep, a work of art

more elegant than nature's crude design. She was encircled
by restraints, eyes covered, wrists and ankles circled
in soft leather, and then like a child herself, led

into fitful slumber. She clawed up to gray morning, birdsong,
cries that might have been anyone's. A soft, ordinary work song
hummed by a masked orderly. And here, they say, your son.

A child born from no place, from the flame of her forgetting,
bracket of blank pages. The boy, too, was destined to forget—
a bird from no tree branch, fish from no river, sword from no forge.

Houma, Louisiana, 1862

"You here, Missus? I cain't see not a thing."
The woman tugged her soft robe around herself
and watched Liza limp up to the porch in the darkness.
"I'm here, Liza," she said, holding out her pale hand.

"You boil that water and get you a cup like I asked?"
The woman, who shook even in the summer evening,
nearly said "Yes ma'am," but caught herself.

Old Liza, clacking her lantern down on the wood,
reminded the woman of a crumbling, ancient goddess,
a dusty sibyl with a spell for every wrong.

But she knew this was not magic, knew all the magic
had dried up from the earth like the streams
in drought. This was the dust left behind.

"Missus, you know now, you know your husband
cain't know about this. You tell him—I'll get strung up
like a windchime. Give me that hot water, now, and your word."

The woman handed Liza the cup of scalding water,
said her promises, pressed her forearms
into her own stomach. Inside, her husband

lay sprawled in the bed, exhausted, no doubt,
from his nightly war on her body. Liza produced
purple flowers ("Pennyroyal, Missus") from her pocket,

shredded the leaves, dropped them in the water to steep.
The woman lifted the cup to her mouth, but Liza,
brown skin shining in the lantern light, grabbed her arm.

"You drink that, ain't no coming back from it. Thing'll be gone
like it never was." The woman's stomach turned,
but she parted her lips and swallowed the tea all at once.

Liza pressed her own lips together and nodded her head.
"I think you a good woman, Missus," she said.
The woman thought the tea might come back up.

"Go on back to your bed, Liza," the woman whispered,
wiping her mouth with her sleeve like a savage.
"He'll never know. You always tell me what you need,

and you'll have it." Liza patted her arm, scooped up
her lantern, and made her way off. The light grew smaller
through the minutes, like a soul with no body
steering the long dry road out of the world.

Mother and Son in Ash

This week,
scientists discovered the remains
of a boy and his mother in Pompeii—
he, still small, curled in her lap,
their arms burnt forever around each other,
some final whisper passed eternally
between them in stone.
They were lifted from the earth, taken
to be cleaned.

The scientists, reports say, wept freely
in the white and sterile hallways.

Nice, France, 1886

In the night, Josephine dreamed of saints and monsters.
St. Gerard's blessed kerchief settled on a dying mother's
belly as she labored, and lo, the baby came, the mother saved.
But then they turned to dragons. The Devil swallowed
St. Margaret whole until she burst from his belly,

the holy birthed from evil. She woke to Grand-Mère's
cold and certain fingers on her ankle. "Come, Josephine. Lamps
and water to the inner room. Arise. We are needed."
Secretly, Grand-Mère was called *Faiseuse D'Anges,*
The Angel Maker, white witch who cast the pebble of a child

into the sky. The girl on the table held out crumpled francs,
face splashed with firelight. She'd been before, raped
by her father, had thrown herself from a terrace to crush
the quickening, but only cracked her jaw which jutted still
to one side. Grand-Mère had let the air in then, swept the thing

away, then laid the ailing girl beside two others in her own bed
to coax her color back. That was last year, before Grand-Mère offered
Josephine an apron, taught her how to tend women,
to watch the basins to be sure they'd got it all. Josephine fainted
the first time. But women came and came, knocked and wept,

swept by tides onto their stoop in the evenings. Women: beautiful
and plain, women who pinched tomatoes in the square,
washed their windows, kept chickens in their yards. Tonight, Josephine
cast kerchiefs and dragons from her head. No space for saints
in these close walls. Grand-Mère, whose children never

thought her tender, hummed as she worked, said,
"Lean, my love. I have you." Her hands worked like whispers
around the bruised legs, the girl grown pale, absent as a ghost.
Grand-Mère spoke to Josephine only with her eyes: *watch for blood,*
say nothing of the father, feel her pulse, stop praying stop
praying. God has no place here. The girl's heart drummed a dirge

at the wrist. Calling on the lineage of witches' wisdom,
Josephine held the just-round belly with a palm, willed
strength into the girl, and then the tissues came. Resting later
in Grand-Mère's bed, the girl mumbled a rosary while Grand-Mère
and Josephine hid the tools, scrubbed the basin, swept the floor before sunrise.

WEAPON

Shorn

1.
The Pentecostal woman next door confides:
the Lord forbids a blade touch her hair. It rats
and scrapes her knees, frayed, unbeautiful.
She weeps in the mornings, rakes and breaks
comb teeth through it. Her neck is off. She whispers,
"The nice gay man downtown says he will take me
out back, douse it with perm solution, and clap it off
between two boards." The Lord, she knows,
is merciful.

2.
Not even God can bear our nakedness
and, in his kindness, curtained us with hair.
Mine is beautiful. I have seen men's fingers,
possessed, clicking and itching to reach for it,
to catch it in a breeze. It is long, golden,
and as God wills it, when I am unclothed,
it covers almost everything that makes me
woman.

With it, imagine all the saviors' feet
I could anoint with precious oil, on my knees
repentant, reborn. Or put in my place,
towered, chaste, think of all the princes
who could grip it like rope in their sweating fists,
scale my prison, unlock me, liberate me
from witches.

3.
In crowded squares, inquisitors shaved witches
bare to seek out the devil's mark. When they found none,
they tried to coax it out, poured boiling lard
into the women's eyes, navels, vaginas. The devil
marks us all.

4.
Unshorn, we are death itself: serpentine
and secret. Our hair conceals our power
to bear souls into the world, to feed them
from our own flesh: sower, tender, reaper,
shepherd, wolf, wool and fur. For our crimes

in Eden, temples, beds, and caves, and back
seats, we have been covered by the gods
in hair, snaked by goddesses, marked by devils,
beheaded by heroes and weaponized.
And still their fingers. Their fingers twitch.
They must know what it feels like in their hands.

5.
Perhaps if we let it loose, pin it up, braid it
in one braid, two braids, corn row it,
perhaps if we perm it, straighten it, relax
it, iron it, perhaps if we pick it into an afro,
perhaps if we shave it, wig it, veil it,
perhaps if we cover it in a habit, so that from the sky,
we are indiscernible from each other,

they will be satisfied.

Perhaps if we pluck it, wax it into triangles
and thin lines, send electrical signals into the follicles,
perhaps if we trade it for food, for money,
for train fare, Christmas presents, perhaps if we
let you snip a lock to worship, perhaps if we
let you wrap it around our necks like nooses

you will be satisfied.

6.
The Russian army found fourteen thousand pounds
of human hair when they took Auschwitz. Bailed
and loose, still curled, ribboned. The hair yet unused
for socks, for mattresses upon which men would dream
of women, for thread,
for rope.

Dublin, Ireland, 1893, 1993

1893
Catherine Grehan, who had only been called "Twenty-Seven"
for years she could not count, woke to bells
in darkness. When she was a girl, men looked at her longer

than others, and so her father hid his too-beautiful
fourth daughter in the laundry. She had never seen a mirror
inside the walls, but doubted her beauty endured.

She dressed in a line of others and silently ate
food left from yesterday. She counted six mouthfuls
—one for each hour until she'd eat again.

The others counted, too. Counted and measured to stay alive—
months measured by blood on the rags, their babies'
ten fingers, two eyes, dozens of dusty eyebrows

thousands of miles away in strangers' cradles
being called the wrong names. Catherine Grehan
was famous, as much as fame could be

measured in the bitter silence, for trying to escape.
Last April when it thawed, she'd scaled the wall
but hadn't counted on the glass along the top.

This morning, she sank her scarred hands for some thousandth time
into the morning's wash, sheets and draperies, stained
and soaked and heavier than many men could lift.

By ten o'clock, the water had gone milky like the priest's skin.
She'd memorized him when he visited her cell, shaved her
head, made her sorry for her pitiful attempt to flee.

His child kicked her lowest rib as she heaved her load
into the rinsing bin. Catherine Grehan, baptized daily
by ice and reborn into hell, knew what did

and did not come clean.

1993
After the nuns of Our Lady of Charity sold their land
to settle bad stock bets, a foreman found the bones.
When the excavators arrived and began their work,

some of the men still believed in God.

They lifted one hundred fifty-five women
and their babies from the ground. Their limbs
were crooked, shattered, plaster-casted. One they found

buried separate from her head.

Work stopped for the day when the youngest man,
who still lived with his mother, found the bones
of a woman, the bones of her baby

cradled inside her broken ribs.

Supply

I pump my breasts
in a campus supply closet. Exposed
pipes rattle in one corner. Grime
from the air-vent blankets piles
of envelopes, letterhead,
a molding mop, a hundred uncapped pens.

A stand holds condiments and off-brand
hand sanitizer, and next to my hard chair
is a shelf of dated textbooks bound
for recycling. Sometimes

to forget I am vacuuming out my son's
first food in a dark windowless cube,
I read: The milk's infused with apples
when I read Frost, salt
for Hemingway. Today,

like the Bible opening to the page
you need, I find Knight
dried out and smoking poems in his single cell—
Bukowski, boxer, scribbling
in the cage of hourly hotels
between jobs and prostitutes.

I don't want to think how they'll taint my milk,
but I cling to the thought of them clawing up beauty
in the grotesque, paint peeling
to reveal some single, lonesome truth.

I write this poem with three-days-dirty
hair, boxing through the seventh
month of heartache and dust,
of iron pills and metered sleep in caves
of blankets, afternoons, no Lexapro, no booze
so the milk stays clean.
The poem creeps up to knock a knuckle
on the bars. The poem knows hunger,
knows there's someone waiting, desperate
to be fed. The poem rushes forth
and, like so many others, would not arrive
without a hell for its return address.

Los Alamos, New Mexico, 1945

Elizabeth Graves walks through a contraction
in a sweltering hotel room with her husband
and a Geiger Counter. The bomb she built,

first of its name, exploded hours ago in the desert,
its outcry faint and soft over the radio.
When they'd hired her husband, promised him

mountains and a name, they hadn't known
the lovelier Dr. Graves. They soon discovered
she was the key. Only a handful of people alive

understood fast neutron scattering. Only a few
could operate the particle accelerator. She could,
who now wills her water not to break.

Her husband exhales on her nape, grips her
thin wristwatch, ever the numbers man.
"How far apart?" he asks her.

She's forgotten the counting. Any moment,
the fallout will register on the machines, and her name
will be born to the future, and cannot be unborn.

Women bravely bear the pain of birth, they say, because
what is the alternative? A man can flee a war,
desert his unit, keep his hands unbloodied,

but we cannot outrun our bodies. A woman bears
down, brute animal, to do the work
of making. The wave of a contraction rises

and she flattens her palms on the table. "Liz?
I have you. I have you. Think of something else.
Think of a name." But all she can think of

is what she will be called when this morning
is flattened onto the pages of history, when mouths
open to name her. Perhaps they will call her Mother.

Hiroshima, Japan, 1945

In the final hours of pregnancy, Yoshiko
has come to understand her skeleton.
To a woman's small hand, the trunks

of great *akamatsu* trees were hard
as stones, but the right breeze bowed their tops.
Bones bent, too. A storm inside her rose, the bark

of her body grew soft, bent outward, making way.
The midwife held her hands for balance
as she crouched over old blankets. Yoshiko screamed.

"Picture something sweet, girl. Think of your man."
Her husband's body, soaked with seawater,
littered the Pacific with a thousand thousand others.

She hadn't loved him, his rough hands, his ugly
fumbling in their bed. He'd struck her once.
He was weak, and it had not hurt. Sending him

to war had not moved her heart. She was able to eat
shishamo again, which he had not liked. He'd never known
about this child. It was hers entirely, hers

for every coming sunrise of her life. "Once more,"
the midwife said. Something splintered
then gave, split her wide. Something slid

between her feet. "A daughter," said the midwife,
swaddling the girl in a torn jacket. A daughter,
thought Yoshiko. Her husband would have grieved.

But inside Yoshiko, a dormant flower
bloomed. The midwife settled the girl in her arms,
and Yoshiko saw her own brows and eyes, tiny, mirrored back.

The baby took her nipple. Daughter, she thought,
as the damp palms searched her breast, as the milk
came. Daughter, she thought, the war is ending.

Daughter, she thought, there will be afternoons
of jasmine, braided hair, simple suppers in the yard.
I will feed you from the garden. Daughter,

she thought, I will ferry you. I will be your cool shade
and your help. I will teach you each live thing's name.
I will name you Asuka: the smell of tomorrow.

I Know God

is not a woman, and it is not the torn silk-flesh
and fire trial of the baby born. Not the bleeding,
not the curse. Not the rib myth,
first sin myth, not the apple's red skin,
which still stops us, glinting, in the market.

It is not our small bodies, brittle bones,
not our skin soft-on-purpose, a life of receiving,
opening legs, allowing, permitting,
bearing thrusts and fists and children
almost alone. I know each day

the earth's eternal mothers wake while God
still dozes in his blankets, sweep the last day's children's bones
into a gentle breeze, light a fire, tend it
a while, leave without pay. I know God is a boy
uncertain of his footing, not only

because of His silence as our bodies burned
on pyres, as our feet were bound, our daughters
sold, not only because of His silence as men in white
dismissed our midwives, called them witches,
cracked our children's skulls with forceps, clipped us.

I know it was a man, God, who asked Abraham to kill
his son. It was a man, Abraham, who said to Him
"How soon? With which blade? Upon
what rock?" Who else lives for sport, a shock of blood—blows
a coach's whistle for time just as the knife nicks?

At night, in shadow, hardheaded goddesses
call spring grasses up from battlefields,
billow rain to rinse the sacrificial rocks,
contract the laboring mother's ribs,
coax and shepherd one more child to life.

Pearl River, Louisiana, 1859

Liza's torn loins, raw, cried-out lips,
swollen eyes were altogether separate
from the soul. Her soul was three days
in its grave with her newborn son, decaying.

Her body endured alone, the dumb animals
of lungs and heart drummed on.
She was sold in a rush while her milk
still flowed, knocked around in a hard wagon

two nights, her dress soaked with cold,
stinking milk, and afterbirth. The body was a fool.
Stubbornly, it made the milk, wouldn't hear
from the heart that the boy was dead.

She'd been bought by a farmer—tobacco thick
in the air, locked in his room—whose wife bled to death
bearing a son. This boy's body was the color
of peach skin, a little yellowed, eyes still closed.

His mother would have called him beautiful.
Liza couldn't look straight at him, motherless
and simple as he was. He only had to smell her
to open his thin white lips and nurse, desperation

dulling in his throat. It had the nerve to be April,
Liza thought, feeding him in the gray shade
of a new morning. Thimbleweed and violets, separate from her,
from the boy, bloomed in the yard. The earth

spoke its mother tongue, easy and familiar with itself,
not slowing for a body that had lost the language.
The boy opened his eyes. Trembling, Liza shifted,
held his skull, looked at him straight on,

felt what God must feel when He tires of us—indifferently
spinning the earth, beaten but afraid of what would happen
if He stopped. Her body alone drew up
some final, weary tenderness, held on to this boy,

alone, and let him have her.

Morning

My child, who has learned kisses,
presses his lips through the crib rails
to meet mine. I rock and nurse him
in the early dark. The day waits.

Later, his father and I each sock and shoe
a tiny foot, double-knot the laces.
The day wakes and says, "Give him
to me. I don't think I'll hurt him."

This morning, as I lift him in the air,
a bomb falls and men who were
boys once exhale forever. This morning,
I teach my son to say "light."

This morning, boys who will be men soon
are lit by bullets in the desert dark.
This morning, I teach my son to say "yes"
and to make ocean sounds.

This morning, the ocean washes up bodies
of children like messages, and I hold my boy
in trembling hands. It feels wicked to love him
this much, to love him at all

on such a ruthless rock as this. But the day
keeps offering up its boys, saying, "Love them,
or return them to the earth." The earth waits,
ready to kiss them with its hungry mouth.

Tehran, Iran, 1941

In his youth, he had left his mother's house
early in the morning, tied on his apron,
and spent hours infusing whipped cream
with roses to garnish the Persian Love Cakes,
triple-sifting chickpea flour for cookies
in the window case. He lived a life

of honey, of nectar, of the sweetest milk until
the English came from below and the Russians
came from above and the war laced its taste
through them all. Then his mother died,
the country curled in on itself in war, and he left
her house early in the morning, tied on his apron
and made rows of plain loaves
to hand out to the starving.

Day they came and night they came. Time
was measured in morning lines and evening lines.
The mind can preserve the smell of rose-laced cream
for such a little time before it goes and is replaced
with gunpowder, dust like flour, blood like batter.
For himself, he forgot it all (the recipes, the sweetness)

the winter night he saw the huddled mother
nursing her baby against the bakery's front steps
long after the crowds had gone. His own mother's
ghost urged him out in the frozen wind
to offer her the last brown roll of bread.
When he came to her, he saw that she had died,
though still, as the snow fell, her child nursed desperately,
determined that this last sweet thing would last the night.

Edenton, North Carolina, 1968

> I was raped twice, once by the perpetrator and
> once by the state of North Carolina.
> —ELAINE RIDDICK, 2012

1.
Maggie Woodard, whom everyone calls
Miss Peaches, watches them wheel
her granddaughter away. They tell her
the girl is feebleminded, too dim to speak
or be reasoned with. They explain
the greater good. Maggie remembers the girl
reading to her from the Bible.
Miracle after miracle.

Maggie cannot read.
She holds the stack of papers
in her lap, pinning the edges
so the fan doesn't scatter them
to the floor. The doctor pinches
the bridge of his nose, impatient,
tells her, "Sign, or you won't get benefits.
Sign or we'll send the girl
to an orphanage." She draws an X
in the white space.

2.
Confidential
Eugenics Board of North Carolina

Petition for Operation of Sterilization or Asexualization

Your petitioner, Mrs. Urusla B. Spruill, Director of Public Welfare, having made a full study of the case of Miss Elaine Riddick, hereinafter designated as the patient,

AND WHEREAS it appears to your Petitioner that (1) it is for the best interest of the mental, moral, and physical improvement of the patient that she undergo an operation for sterilization; (2) that it is for the public good that such patient undergo such operation; (3) that said patient would be likely to procreate a child or children who would have a tendency to serious physical, mental, or nervous disease or deficiency;

NOW THEREFORE Your Petitioner prays that an order be entered by the Eugenics Board of North Carolina requiring your Petitioner to perform, or to have performed by some competent surgeon upon Miss Elaine Riddick, the patient named in this Petition, the operations specified in Section 36, Chapter 35, of the General Statutes of North Carolina, which in the discretion of the Board, shall be best suited to the interests of said patient or to the public good.

3.
The doctor scrubs his arms
to the elbow, fingers filing between fingers.
Yesterday, he'd saved a twelve-year-old negro girl
who talked too much about boyfriends.
The day before, a moron woman
who'd wandered to the woods
to bear her child.

Such mercies had he doled
to thousands, and how many
tens of thousands had been spared
their brutal, simple lives in turn?
He warms as the nurse slides
the gloves on, loves the pop they make
when she releases, loves the sight of the blade
in his hand, a baton with which he might conduct
the music of all human voices,
all human noise.

4.
The year before, Elaine had been kidnapped
by a man on her street. His fingernails
were stained with grease. His house smelled
like newsprint and food gone bad. A fly
had buzzed to the dirty carpet
and watched,
the only witness.

This morning, fourteen years old
and two days in labor, she breathes
their gas and air. They numb her,
cut her
open, and hand her a son.
She doesn't feel the other cut.
The doctor smiles
as he stitches. Hums.
This is the cleanest room she has ever seen.

Nunavik Region, Quebec, Canada, 1965

Since Yuka had come to love the boy Tupiq,
words had dissolved, useless, many times
in her mouth. *Young* and *small,* for instance.

Tupiq was younger, smaller. But when she spoke this,
it was a lie. He was fearsome unclothed,
his hands and shoulders infused with the wisdom

of his grandfathers. But even Tupiq the fearsome
could not stop the helpers—another wrong word—
Qallunaat: white people who came to steal women

with child. Yuka had seen them helping many times.
In the mothers' ninth moon, the *Qallunaat*
descended and swept the women away on planes

to southern hospitals. Yuka's sister's child died
inside her the first time.
"Your midwives are untrained," they said.

"Our doctors went to school. This is the better way."
They left the women in stark motels with battered Bibles
and phonebooks in the drawers. They called it "killing time."

Tupiq woke Yuka in the night, wrapped her
in his furs, and hid her in the *Aanigutyak,*
the hut where children should be born.

He is young, after all, Yuka thought, but she let him
hide her, let him stroke her belly under her clothes,
let him feed her from his hand one last time

before the planes came and then there would be
only lukewarm food on plastic plates. Love, too,
was a useless word for this, the charged space

between their bodies—*akkunaptingni*. "I will return,"
she spoke into his shoulder as the baby rolled
to the drum of their mating. She fell asleep and dreamed

the baby came in the night—here as it should:
her mother between her legs, Tupiq singing old music,
the days after in her own clothes. But they were discovered

by the helpers early in the morning. The *Qallunaat*
peeled the lovers apart as if skinning an animal,
although, Yuka knew, almost laughing, they would not

know how. All of their animals
lived in cages and died far away
from the rest of their kind.

Montgomery, Alabama, 1847

He didn't bother anymore with draping a sheet
over Anarcha's open knees, had never bothered
to soothe her, crack open ether, look at her eyes.

The child was long dead who'd torn open
the two rivers of her body so that filth trickled always
down her legs. The doctor bought her

for a bargain when word spread of her affliction,
tossed her in with twelve others, all torn by babies
or his knife in one swift flick. Today, the twentieth

time he'd splayed her on this table, he strapped
on his mask to guard against the smell, unpacked the cobwebs
from her wound, dropped them in kerosene. She decided

to speak to her ancestors. He opened her
with two cold spoons, and her blood pounded through
generations, girlhoods in tall grass, sun

through the window dappling the heads of dead women,
her baby somewhere handed between them.
Grandmothers, she thought,

breaking her nails on the table as he loosed
the old stitches, *damn your steps. Curse your kissing
mouths, your daughters being born and bearing*

daughters. Damn the daughters.
He did not even trouble anymore
to tell her what a service was her suffering, how fine

ladies in the future, thus afflicted, would think of her
with thanks. He would etherize them, she knew.
He would drape their white bodies in linen and they would dream.

He cut a fresh line, hummed, stitched. She smelled
herself. *Grandmothers, make ready,* she thought she howled
out loud. *Damn the ether. Plant the demons*
in the soil of every fine white wound
he stitches. Let your curse rattle before them,
behind them, odorous, memorial.

Buenos Aires, Argentina, 1978

> They presented a truly sickening combination—the
> curiosity of little boys, the intense arousal of twisted men.
> —Statement of anonymous detainee, ESMA Camp

1.
Before she was taken by the *junta,* chained,
hooded, she had seen on television that NASA
had launched the Viking 1 into orbit.
Four months of blackness made her believe
she understood space: vacuous, vacant,

an enclosure of silence, voice a blunt, useless
tool. The baby has begun to move, a soft rapping
that reminded her of her husband throwing pebbles
at her window when they were young,
each little thump a question: will you love me?

When they'd shot him in the night, Viking
somewhere above them, she closed instantly,
locked and sealed the doorways of her body.
The baby kicks hard, and she jerks at her chains,
desperate to touch her own belly, to stop it.

Will you love me? Will you love me?

2.
The man who killed her husband comes in the night,
kicks her awake. The others call him the Blond Angel of Death,
but he smiles at her as he washes her face,
tells her to call him Alfredo. He gives her
a dead woman's dress to wear, makes her

say thank you. Later, in an opulent restaurant
where she must eat food from his fork, must kiss him,
he says, "Isn't this wonderful? Aren't you happy
to be clean? You look so nice. I bet you were beautiful
once." Some part of his body is always touching her.

Later, every part of his body is touching her
as he leads her in a waltz. She is clumsy
with the baby's weight. Everyone watching
must believe the child is his. He has a knife
pressed into the folds of her dress.
He doesn't need it.

3.
The naval cadets have been drinking, gotten brave,
so they remove her hood. They let her look
at the the generator, bronze spoon, wire wrapped roughly
around the handle, before they put it inside her.
For a long time after, the baby does not move.

Don't die, she whispers to it when they are finally
alone, although dying feels sensible, the only right choice
left. The guards are good Catholics, would never kill
a pregnant woman. *I keep you alive,* she says,
rocking her hips back and forth, wincing,

and you keep me alive. It is a command. In the darkness,
she begins compiling opposites: the opposite of boys is not girls,
but men. The opposite of death is pregnancy. The opposite
of war is space travel. The opposite of war is pebbles
on the window. The opposite of war is birth.

SHIP

Missoula, Montana, 1950

Dot sighed and pushed her cart, burdened with Lux Flakes
on sale and the Ritz Crackers her husband liked
crumbled on his casseroles. Her son giggled

in the cart, trying to disappear beneath the boxes.
A routine fog dulled her thoughts, his laughter
sweet but muted, as if an aisle away.

She shook loose, straightened her dress, pushed
the boy and his boxes past the cake flour
and frozen TV dinners to the back wall stacked

with little jars of baby food. While her husband Jim spoon fed
the boy on Saturday mornings as Popeye played,
he loved booming, "Look at the boy,

meat on his bones!" She found herself
working to muster a smile at the thought
when another cart stopped short on the same row.

"Dot," said June Polcek, color spotting her pale cheek. Dot loved
the faded blue dress June wore, remembered
ironing it once early in the morning, holding it against her face.

She braced, shifted her weight. Her hands flitted
around her own clothes as if confirming their presence.
"Hello, June," she replied, dropping the Gerber jars

into the basket and reaching out a gloved hand to shake.
June reached over her pregnant belly and took it.
They touched like strangers, acquaintances from church,

Dot thought, scanning for other shoppers' eyes.
But Dot had known those hands, known each knuckle. Frozen
there, fingers fixed in June's, Dot did not resist

the memory of another time when both their palms
were calloused from mill work they'd assumed while their husbands
were at war. Their hands were like a baby's now,

uncertain, underused. "How far along?" she asked,
when what she ought to say was, "Come away,
the babes and all." She swallowed this whole.

June smiled, smelled it on the air. "Just another month."
She slid Dot's hand on her belly without asking,
drawing her whole body forward. Their gazes met, unwavering.

Dot's son fidgeted in the cart, restless. Her tears tickled
the creases of her cheeks as she stood, flanked by bright cereal boxes,
pulverized, jarred food, fluorescent lights, body trapped

in starched clothes, touching the woman she had touched
so often once, the woman she had whispered to, woken nightly,
the radio mumbling its bad news in the next room.

The Thing They Say Makes Us
Love Each Other

The first time I told him "I want to be dead,"
many years ago, I meant it.
I pictured the pills on the nightstand—
each one a rounded stair I'd climb.

The bottle bore my name,
but it was the name my mother chose,
the name no one uses: Katherine.
He calls me Kate

and maybe that is why I'm still alive.
Maybe that is why I let him lead me
into the yard and sit me in the sun
and ask me not to die

and I didn't. When the boy won't come
after two days, he walks me down
the hospital's white hallways
with the calm certainty of a man

who has navigated a woman many times
through her own darknesses.
When the boy won't come after three days,
and there is little left

between me and the knife,
the doula whispers in his ear
that oxytocin (the thing they say
makes us love each other)

can bring contractions.
She tells him how and leaves us
alone in the dark room, guards
the door to keep the nurses out. He licks

his fingers and dips his hand between my legs
the way he has a thousand times.
I remember the first time he did this.
I was shocked that another's hand

could find a truth in my body
I had missed. Now, as then, he looks at me,
imploring, with something simpler than love.
He strokes me and watches the monitor,

marvels at the peaks and valleys he creates,
and I think, as my body obeys,
This is the center of the universe,
the lamp-lit island between living and dying.

These are waters he knows well.
At last, my labor speeds. I scream,
"I can't. I want to die," and it's truer
than before—an urgency to flee

the sinking ship of my body,
to be expelled into the vacuum of space,
to drown silently in cold water.
The room has filled with women,

chuckling. "Wanting to die means it's time,"
they tell us, and it begins. *He knows,* I want to say.
He married a woman sad in her bones.
He knows the thrill and rest after I choose to live

*one more time, the months or years after
smooth and light like fresh skin after a burn.*
He stands between my legs, and we ship death
away—maybe forever. And now, there is a boy

in my arms. Is this what all the afternoons
of my life, curled around a question,
were for? Is this, the moment that I finally
ask someone else to live for me,

the secret he has always wanted me to know?

Shreveport, Louisiana, 1986

The woman's gangling teenaged sons had been sent
to stay with friends, husband to hunt deer. Dreamily,
she wiped counters, and all at once, the ladies came.

Marabella and Dancia and their Great Aunt Mae,
the women she had loved as girls and their daughters
and mothers and sisters until the kitchen was pregnant
with Catholics and a twenty-pound goose.

At thirty-six, there were no guarantees for babies,
and less than none for girls. But Aunt Mae, all knuckles
and cataracts, knew recipes for everything—even, she said,
girlchildren late in life. All day, the bird roasted

and the women basted, said rosaries, chopped garlic
and laughed at jokes in bad taste. They painted nails
and laid healing hands on the woman's belly,

spoke to Mother Mary and their ancestors and
the ghosts of women who had lived there before.
Sun dripped out of the windows, candles came,
sistersongs and red wine saved for just these days.

They ate the sacrificial meat, loved each other, said farewell.
They'd find out soon: Aunt Mae's magic took.
A spell-born daughter quickened, made her way.

Plea

In the fourth month of his life,
the boy has learned to sleep. One room over,
his mother curls in her own bed, still
body-braced for a cry, but only white noise
rain sounds feather down the corridor.

She holds her own body under blankets,
hips and ribs thinned back down,
belly a stark, lonely plane. No knuckles
knock to be released. No body
rolls in slow response to her sighs.

Her eyes flicker open, closed.
The room fills and empties like a lung.
He sleeps.
Please, she mouths to the thin dark,
please, baby. Please. Cry out.

Serengeti District, Tanzania, 2017

for Rhobi Samwelly, The Angel of Mugumu

On the third day of her confinement in the locked room,
Afya has begun to see ghosts: her sister, Faida, white blood
trickling down her thighs, drifts near to her and sings soft songs.

It is cutting season, and some demon had climbed in Afya's mouth
and she spat her refusal at her father. He'd laughed.
"You are worthless uncut, girl. The ten cows of dowry

will pay for your brother's schooling." When she again refused,
he broke her ribs with his boot and bolted her in the store room.
"I am going for the circumciser now," he'd raged and disappeared.

Her sister's ghost kisses her hands. They had pinned Faida
near a fire. Her grandmothers held her arms, her mother her legs.
She struggled so fiercely the ball of her shoulder sprang loose.

The knife man, paid his price, sliced her with a sharp hot stone
from pubic bone to anus down each side. She was sewn and her knees
bound together. Days after, when her urine stalled, she stole glass

from a shattered window and, in a frenzy, cut herself open.
They buried her in the bush and never spoke her name. Footsteps.
Afya blew the ghost away and stilled herself. She would fight

the knife man, too, struggle until both shoulders broke. She'd break
her teeth on his bones. She'd die, too, but not without his blood.
The footsteps neared. The bolt unhooked and Afya shielded her eyes.

But when the voice said "Girl," it was her mother's, whispering.

She wrapped Afya's fingers around a sack made from an old dress.
"Run to the bush," she said, crushing Afya into her chest.
"I've called the woman from Mugumu. She will keep you until the season ends.

You must run. They will follow you. It takes seven minutes
to run a kilometer. You must run north for three hours, until the woman comes."
Her mother knelt and kissed Afya's soft feet. "Your feet will bleed.

And heal." Afya began to cry. Her mother rose and shook her.
Faida's ghost paced beyond the open door, waiting.
"But mother, what about the cows?" she asked.

"A boy can always find another way," her mother said,
and kissed her hard, and shoved her out into the rain.
The girl and the ghost ran silently, north into the night.

Unnamed Hamlet, Oaxaca, Mexico, 2004

Ines' eighth baby died inside her.
Her waters long broken, she was too far
from town, from the doctor, from the knife
she needed to rescue the child from herself.
It struggled at the end, then stilled, drowned
just as it glimpsed the shore it knew it would never reach.

Tonight, another child threatens its own death,
pressing hopelessly down between her legs
and will not come. Her husband is far away
in *el campo* cutting illegal lumber. No matter.
He could not save her anyway. "Benito!"
she screams to her eight-year-old son.

He comes, solemn and steady. She presses
her last coins into his hand, tells him to buy a sharp knife
from the tiny shop in the next village. The boy,
who has seen death before, runs too fast to see.
Ines rocks back and forth on her knees, remembering
the child who had lived and stopped living in her body.

Grief felt like contractions in reverse. First, it came
in waves so close together that they all seemed like one
long storm, one that would level a woman. Then,
as time went on, as the welcome burden of everyday things
returned, the waves spread out. She would be pounding corn
and feel it coming, feel it rise, peak, sting her, and ease away.

The baby thrashed under her navel and she knew
that she would die. By candlelight, she lay against
the wall of her rough, empty house and tipped
homemade *mezcal* back into her throat. Benito returned.
"Mama, a knife," he said, closing her fingers around it.
"Take the others away," she croaked. "Find help."

When she was alone, she finished off the liquor, spat the worm,
and pictured every pig she'd slaughtered in her life.
Flesh was flesh, animal muscle, vessels and veins.
She leaned back and pushed her hips forward
so her womb was pressed against her skin. The child kicked
and she opened herself. The blood was black

in the low light. She cut again. She cut three times,
hands slipping, screamed, and went limp. Her intestines fell warm
outside her, blood like a blanket. But then the dead boy's fingers ghosted
across her brow, and she recalled the unmoving weight
of him, the cold stone of her child who never breathed.
She inhaled and found the thin film of her uterus, gripped the knife.

She slit her uterus and found the child's ankle, pulled him
into the world. He cried. He cried and she inhaled it like a drug.
She named him, had barely time to love him, and she lay him
at her side, sliced the cord that joined them, and began
pressing her organs back inside her the best she could.
Her vision flickered in and out. The candle died in the night.

Later, after the tailor came and sewed her, after she was carried
in the hills to a lorry, her insides still contracting, after the hours
in the dark, after the doctor at last, she saw the boy open his eyes
and knew it would be a long time before grief would visit her again,
knew that her body, which had been a coffin, an ocean, a tomb,
was also a doorway, a candle, a weapon, a ship.

At Last, She Is Finished with Emptiness

After slow months of healing, night
nursing, the breast pump, burying
the old, faithful dog, board meetings, cursing
the monitor, the hurrying, three-minute showers
and half-hour naps and instant breakfasts,
finally, her husband who can wait

no longer leads her up the worn stairs
to the sanctuary of rumpled bedding. He guides her
mouth onto him, tilts her backwards,
reopens her softly, a storm door creaking
in sunlight after long darkness. She hears the crack
of a bat; a crowd cheers at the ballpark

down the street. She imagines the sweating
fans cheer for her, that the jays and robins
herald her coming, that she is being urged,
egged on by the whole waking universe. Yes. At last,
she is saying yes again, summering, ready again
to belong to the boy and to the man.

Afterwards, she tells him a year's worth
of secrets. Then they hear the blankets rustle,
a babble over the monitor. Sirens sing
their songs from both sides, to hold them
there, to make them rise, promise such silence
and noise and thirst and wetness, more than enough.

ACKNOWLEDGMENTS

Versions of the following poems have been previously published:

"At Last, She is Finished with Emptiness" in *The Missouri Review* 40.2; "Charleston, South Carolina, 1864" in *The Southern Quarterly* 54.2; "Dublin, Ireland, 1893, 1993" in *Radar,* issue 16; "Hiroshima, Japan, 1945" in *Frontier;* "Houma, Louisiana, 1862" in *The Belle Mar;* "Los Alamos, New Mexico, 1945" in *The Missouri Review* 40.2; "Magdeburg, Germany, 1912" in *The Missouri Review* 40.2; "Missoula, Montana, 1950" in *Radar,* issue 16; "Montgomery, Alabama, 1847" in *Radar,* issue 16; "Nice, France, 1886" in *The Missouri Review* 40.2; "Nunavik Region, Quebec, Canada, 1965" in *Radar,* issue 16; "Pearl River, Louisiana, 1859" in *The Southern Quarterly* 54.2; "Shorn" in *New Millennium Writings* 2017, winner of the 43rd New Millennium Poetry Prize; "Supply" in *Bared: Contemporary Poetry and Art on Bras and Breasts* from Les Femmes Folles Press; "Tehran, Iran, 1941," in *The Missouri Review* 40.2; "The Good News" in *The New Guard,* vol. IV; and "Unnamed Hamlet, Oaxaca, Mexico, 2004" in *Radar,* issue 16.

SOURCE MATERIALS

Most of the poems in this book would not exist without the work of others—particularly wonderful investigative journalists, devoted academics, and career historians. Some of the poems are composites of the stories of many women, especially in cases where records of the events in question were lost or intentionally destroyed. For example, a huge number of birth and death records of women and children kept against their will in Magdalene Laundries in Ireland were destroyed or altered. Sometimes, this was done so that babies given away for adoption could not be traced back to their mothers; sometimes it was done because the mothers and babies had died and the laundries did not want to be held liable. My composite uses the name of a real mother who died in the Our Lady of Charity laundry. When mass graves of bones were found, hers were assumed to be among them but, of course, could not be identified.

In the cases of Anarcha and other enslaved and indentured women living in the American South, we only have records insofar as they were kept by the women's white male owners. Having Anarcha's name and medical history is, in and of itself, a rarity among such cases. I tried to use composites as responsibly as possible, and to pull details only when I found them confirmed by more than one woman's account. The story of the woman in Pearl River, for example, was a brutally common tale: a black woman who had lost her infant or was forcibly separated from it in order that she might nurse a white baby.

Some of the stories here are factual through and through. The accounts in the poems from Edenton, Tehran, Los Alamos, and Oaxaca, for example, are pulled directly from court records, interviews with the individuals, medical records, and diaries. One lesson I have learned writing this book is how valuable and precious women's own memories are when they are able to record them themselves. When I found an account of an incredible story that a woman had written about her own experience, I felt my heart pound with gratitude. So many of our stories are swallowed, covered up, or stolen. When we are able to protect them by telling them, we have done a service to our daughters through the generations.

Finally, I feel that I should say that the heart of this book—an attempt to tell a kind of monomyth of female struggle, suffering, and victory through time and around the globe—presented the obvious challenge of my own limited identity. I am white. I have never been enslaved, indentured, or discriminated against because of my race. While I have suffered sexual assault, it has been nothing like that of the characters and real women in these poems. I have never lived in poverty. I have never lived through a war in my own country. The list goes on. This is to say, I have lived a privileged life by most modern measures. I have heard and participated in criticism of white writers who, by coopting and telling the stories of people of color, disrupt or entirely displace writers of color who would rather tell their own stories.

That has never left my mind as I wrote these poems. I can say with confidence that no single woman, no matter her race, could ever really hope to sum up the grand narrative of women's struggling and prevailing. I certainly haven't. But I have been a woman, and I have seen the threads of my womanhood sewn backwards through time. I have seen our connections, however fragile and fragmented, through war, discrimination, misogyny, rape, death, nursing, and birth. As I wrote this book, a single image returned and returned: a string of women, all touching each other in some way, circling the globe. I tried, earnestly and imperfectly, to trace that circle. I tried to center the stories that have been decentered for too long, to amplify what has been ignored, to restore what has been erased.

Works to Which I am Generally Indebted:

Randi Hutter Epstein, M.D. *Get Me Out: A History of Childbirth from the Garden of Eden to the Sperm Bank*. W. W. Norton & Company, 2010.

Jennifer Grayson. *Unlatched: The Evolution of Breastfeeding and the Making of a Controversy.* Harper Collins, 2016.

John M. Riddle. *Eve's Herbs: A History of Contraception and Abortion in the West*. Harvard University Press, 1999.

Richard W. Wertz and Dorothy C. Wertz. *Lying In: A History of Childbirth in America*. Yale University Press, 1977.

Sources for Individual Poems (in order of appearance):

"Nice, France, 1886": Rachel G. Fuchs. "Angel Makers (Faiseuses d'Anges) of the Quartier Notre-Dame des Champs: Community and Personal Networks in 1870s Paris." *Genre & Histoire* 17 (2016). http://journals.openedition.org/genrehistoire/2430

"Dublin Ireland, 1893, 1993": Susan Daily. "A Life Unlived: 35 Years of Slavery in a Magdalene Laundry." *The Journal,* 2012. http://www.thejournal.ie/magdalene-laundry-true-story-margaret-bullen-samantha-long-614350-Sep2012/

"The Coverup at High Park Magdalene Laundry, Dublin." *Child Laundering Secrets,* 2017. https://www.childlaunderingsecrets.com/articles/high-crimes-of-mass-murder-at-high-park-magdalene-laundry-dublin

"Los Alamos, New Mexico, 1945": "Elizabeth Riddle Graves." *Atomic Heritage Foundation.* https://www.atomicheritage.org/profile/elizabeth-riddle-graves.

"Tehran, Iran, 1941": Brandon Stanton. *Humans of New York*, August 30, 2015.

"Edenton, North Carolina, 1968": David Zucchino. "Sterilized by North Carolina, She Felt Raped Once More." *Los Angeles Times*, January 25, 2012.

"Montgomery, Alabama, 1847": Shankar Vendantam. "Remembering Anarcha, Lucy, and Betsey: The Mothers of Modern Gynecology." *Hidden Brain: NPR*, February 16, 2016.

"Buenos Aires, Argentina, 1978": Marguerite Feitlowitz. *A Lexicon of Terror:Argentine and the Legacies of Torture*. Oxford University Press, 1998.

"Nunavik Region, Quebec, Canada, 1965": Van Wagner et al. "Reclaiming Birth, Health, and Community: Midwifery in the Inuit Village of Nunavik Canada." *Journal of Midwifery and Women's Health* 52.4 (2007): 384–91.

"Serengeti District, Tanzania, 2017": Sarah Mwambalaswa. "Female Genital Mutilation Practice in Tanzania." Mzumbe University Tanzania, May 2006. *https://www.researchgate. net/publication/237724220_Female_Genital_Mutilation_Practice_in_Tanzania*; Radhika Sanghani "Meet the Amazing Woman Running a Safe House for Girls Fleeing FGM." *The Telegraph*. 4.2 (2015). http://www.telegraph.co.uk/women/womens-health/11509843/FGM-Meet-the-amazing-woman-saving-girls-in-Tanzania.html

"Unnamed Hamlet, Oaxaca, Mexico, 2004": András Szabó. "Auto-Caesarean Section: A Review of 22 Cases." *Arch Womens Mental Health* 17 (2014): 79–83; Ronald Buchanan and Keith Dannemiller. "I Put the Knife In and Pulled it Up. Once Wasn't Enough. I Did It Again. Then I Cut Open My Womb." *The Telegraph*, April 25, 2004. http://www.telegraph.co.uk/news/worldnews/centralamericaandthecaribbean/mexico/1460240/I-put-the-knife-in-and-pulled-it-up.-Once-wasnt-enough.-I-did-it-again.-Then-I-cut-open-my-womb.html

Additional Notes

"The Good News": A Shreveport news station, KSLA News 12, made a kind of music video of "The Good News." It circulated around the globe and was viewed tens of thousands of times, and it still available to view on Facebook on KSLA's page.

"Manhattan, New York, 1970": Nursing has gone through many peaks and valleys as a practice. During and after the World Wars, women entered the workforce and stayed there, which necessarily complicated the nursing relationship as breast pumps were not yet an entirely viable option. Additionally, with the rise of hospital birth and the decline of midwifery in the US, breastfeeding rates were at a record low in the 1960s.

"Serengeti District, Tanzania, 2017": Those wishing to donate to support the Mugumu Safe House (run by Rhobi Samwelly) which provides a refuge for girls fleeing or recovering from female genital mutilation may donate directly by visiting mugumusafehouse.wordpress.com.

CPSIA information can be obtained
at www.ICGtesting.com
Printed in the USA
LVHW041733120419
613991LV00004B/393/P